The Clix the Cat Cyber Safety Series

CLIX THE CAT

Password Chaos

BOOK 1

By Jayme Simmons

ChronoCipher Media

Clix the Cat: Password Chaos

ISBN: 978-1-972486-01-6
Written by Jayme Simmons
Published by ChronoCipher Media
First Edition
Illustrations created with the assistance of AI-based digital illustration tools.
Printed in the United States of America

Part of the Clix the Cat Cyber Safety Series

Also from Jayme Simmons

Malware Monster Mythology

The Cyber Ghost Crew!

The Cyber Time Tracker Series

Follow Codey and Cypher as they travel through time to face the biggest digital threats in history. Each adventure helps young readers learn how technology works—and how smart choices help keep the digital world safe.

Book 1 — Codey's Malware Mission
Book 2 — Codey and the Speed of Worms
Book 3 — Codey and the Phishing Phantoms
Book 4 — Codey vs. the Ransomware Lock
Book 5 — Codey Battles the Botnet

Look for Clix the Cat in his own cyber safety stories.

Clix the Cat tapped his screen again.

"Another password? Seriously?"

He sighed. "I'll just use my favorite one."

Email:
CLIX123
Email:
CLIX123
PASSWORD SETUP
CLIX123
password:
Games:
CLIX123
Bank:
CLIX123

Clix grabbed a pen,

"I'll write it down, just real quick!"

"No one will see it," he said with a grin,

"It's safe on my desk,

I'll just tuck it right in."

PASSWORD:
CLIX123

Far away, something shifted in the digital realm.

It didn't take much.

When passwords are left out in the open,

small problems start to grow.

And time begins to wobble.

10101
1 0101 01
010

With a tick and a tock and a glowing swirl,

A calm, cool figure stepped out of the whirl.

Clix leapt back fast,

his tail went stiff!

“Who are you?! Did I cause... this?!”

She held up her hand with a calm, steady grin,

“Easy there Clix, just breathe for a spin.

I’m not here to scold or say you’re in trouble,

My name’s Cypher and I defend the digital realm.

My ChronoCipher hourglass glows when choices cause trouble. It brought me here.”

"I watch over moments,

what's gone and what's next,

when choices get tricky, time sends a signal.

That password you wrote and left out today,

sent ripples through systems in a risky way."

PASSWORD:

"Some lessons are clearer when seen,"

said Cypher, her voice soft and keen.

"Come with me, Clix just one short peek,

at what can happen in one little week."

In a blink, they arrived at a place full of screens,

where passwords were shared

and locks were nowhere between.

A door blinked unlocked with a quiet blue glow,

And data slipped out, soft, silent, and slow.

They peeked through time at a bright little screen,

where Clix tried to log in, just like he'd been.

He typed his password, quick as could be,

but the screen blinked back,

"Try Again, Kitty!"

Try Again, Kitty!

Clix blinked and he frowned, "But that was my key!

I didn't change it, how could this be?"

Cypher nodded, spoke softly, calm and polite,

"When secrets aren't hidden, they don't stay

secret."

Clix rubbed his chin and his ears tilted back

"I didn't know passwords could travel, so

someone saw it?"

Cypher nodded.

"One small shortcut opened a door.

And doors can open more doors."

Cypher smiled gently, “Passwords are keys,

not notes on a desk for anyone’s eyes to see.

Written on desks, they’re easy to see.

Some secrets are safer when kept quietly.

That’s the safest thing a smart cat can do.”

On a glowing screen, they watched.

A stranger typed the same password.

Email.

Games.

Even the bank.

The same key worked everywhere.

EMAIL
INBOX CLEANED!
BANKING
ACCOUNTS UNLOCKED!
BALANCE:
GAMES
ALL LEVELS UNLOCKED
SYSTEM BYPASSED
ALL ACCOUNTS UNLOCKED
DATA ACCESSED
SECURITY OVERRIDDEN
SOCIAL
MESSAGES
STORE

Clix's whiskers trembled.

"That was supposed to be safe..."

Cypher's voice stayed steady.

"When one key fits every lock,

It's not protection, it's a shock."

"You wouldn't use one house key

for every door in town," she said.

"Passwords work the same way.

Each place deserves its own unque key."

One by one,

digital doors blinked open.

Quiet.

Quick.

Unnoticed.

What felt small

was growing wide.

"What seems tiny can travel far.

A little crack can open wide."

Clix stared at the glowing screens.

He finally understood.

Clix gave a nod and stood up tall,

"I think I know what to do after all."

"No notes, no peeking, no leaving them around,

I'll keep my password safe and sound."

“So what do I do?” Clix asked.

Cypher smiled.

“Long passwords.

Unique passwords.

And never leave them in sight.”

Clix followed Cypher back through the swirling portal and walked straight to his desk.

password
CLIX123

Clix removed the sticky from his desk and started

creating different passwords for his most

important internet sites.

Cypher nodded, “That’s the smartest way.

Strong passwords are special,

one for each place.

Not reused.

Not repeated.

Not left out in sight.”

Clix grinned.

“Okay... shouting them is probably not right.”

Cypher raised an eyebrow.

“Definitely not right.”

Clix scratched his head.

“I used one tiny word for every site.

Easy to remember...

but not very right.”

PASSWORD123
PASSWORD123
PASSWORD123
PASSWORD123
PASSWORD123

Cypher leaned in with a knowing grin,

"So tell me, Clix... what's the fix?"

Clix stood up tall, his eyes shining bright,

"Strong passwords for each place,

and never reuse them, day or night!

No shortcuts!"

Cypher smiled as the ChronoCipher gleamed,

"You've learned what strong passwords really mean.

One for each place, strong and new,

not weak, not reused, just known to you.

No notes, no sharing, no shortcuts, Clix.

You've mastered the rule... and that's the fix."

With a tick and a tock and a shimmering swirl,

Cypher stepped back through the glowing whirl.

The room grew quiet. The portal was gone.

Clix stretched and smiled, the evening rolled on.

Then —PING!

went a message, flashy and sweet:

FREE CAT TREATS! Click here to eat!

Clix's paw hovered over the glowing link.

His ears perked up. He stopped to think...

"Hmm," he murmured, paw held mid-air,

"That looks... amazing."

He blinked.

"How unsafe can free be?"

FREE
CAT
TREATS!

Who is Clix?

Clix is a clever cat who loves shortcuts.
If there is a faster way, easier way, Clix will try it first.

What makes Clix... Clix?

- He trusts too easily
- He learns the hard way
- He doesn't mean to cause chaos... it just happens

Clix's Rule: *"I'll probably be fine!"*

Fun Fact: Clix doesn't try to break the internet, he just makes small choices that turn into big problems.

Who is Cypher?

Cypher is a Time-Travel Defender of the Digital Realm.

She protects the past, present, and future of technology.

What does Cypher do?

- Guides Clix through making better cyber decisions
- Explains big cyber ideas in simple ways
- Keeps missions on track when things get dangerous

Cypher's Rule: *"Knowledge is the strongest defense."*

Fun Fact: Cypher doesn't fight threats directly, she helps others learn how to stop them.

The ChronoCipher hourglass

The ChronoCipher is Cypher's powerful hourglass.

What's inside? Along with sand, it holds glowing 1s and 0s (binary!)

What does it do?

- Controls time travel for Cypher
- Only empties when the lesson is learned
- When the last bit falls, Clix must return home

REMEMBER

Core Lesson of Book 1: Protect Passwords

Small shortcuts can cause big problems.
Smart password habits keep the chaos away.

Made in United States
North Haven, CT
05 November 2026

21765516R00029